49 TIPS FOR A SUCCESSFUL ACCOUNTING CAREER

BY MARK GOLDMAN, CPA

ILLUSTRATIONS BY MICHAEL HILLANBRAND

Library of Congress Cataloging-in-Publication Data
Mark Goldman
49 Tips for a Successful Accounting Career

Library of Congress Control Number: 2018947287
ISBN: 978-1-942923-34-3

49 TIPS FOR A SUCCESSFUL ACCOUNTING CAREER

DEDICATION

I dedicate this book to my father,
Clark S. Goldman, CPA

My Dad, by far, had the most significant influence on my career. Although he would have been happy for me to do anything I enjoyed, he set the stage for me to be able to become an accountant and pass the CPA exam relatively easily.

He was a loving, encouraging man. Although I thought that working for him through middle school, high school, and college was just part of being in a family with a self-employed accountant, he used the situation to immerse me in the career in such a way that accounting just became natural for me. Graduating college courses and later passing the exam was almost a given.

I'm not sure I ever communicated how much I appreciated him before my father passed, but I think he knew. I love you, Dad, and I appreciate what you did to ensure I was able to have a successful, fulfilling, and happy career. Thank you.

ACKNOWLEDGMENTS

I wanted to include a thank-you page in this book because there is absolutely no way that I could have arrived at this point without help.

First, I thank God for placing all the people and resources that I needed to complete this project in my path.

Thank you to Sayuki Goldman, my extraordinary wife, for always supporting me and being the voice of wisdom in my life.

Thank you to Mark Villareal, another author and former co-worker, for being willing to share your publishing knowledge with me.

Thank you to Mike Hillanbrand for completing so much graphic arts work for me over the years, including the illustrations in this book.

Thank you to both Rebeca Garcia and Tricia Barton for being good friends, as well as a proofreaders for this book.

Thank you to Alicia Maples, my business coach for many years, for all of your insight and wonderful ideas for all of our businesses.

And definitely a big thank you to all of our guests for the "Life In Accounting" podcast. I have learned so much from all of our conversations.

I am sure I have missed several people I should be thanking, and I am truly sorry for that.

I appreciate you all!

INTRODUCTION

I decided to write this book a few months after starting a career-related podcast for accountants. Through my interviews, I became the benefactor of extraordinarily fantastic advice from successful individuals in various facets of accounting—people I admired. As we recorded each podcast, my guests would share nuggets of hard-earned wisdom for the benefit of our listeners. In the process, I began to gain insight into my own career journey and life.

This book is a collection of some of the insights I've gained from my guests, as well from my own experience. Over the years, I have had the good fortune of assisting thousands of accountants with their careers. Many of the tips I share here would seem to apply primarily to new accountants, or those in the early stages of their careers, but I believe we can all benefit from hearing some of the basics repeated from time to time. What a difference it would make if we could all remember everything we once knew!

I hope you find this book beneficial and refer to it every few years, because it's likely that a few tips may speak volumes to you now, and the ones that seem like common sense may seem much more insightful under future circumstances. To listen to our podcast, search for "Life In Accounting" on your favorite podcast app, or find us online at www.WhereAccountantsGo.com.

I wish you the best in your career!

MARK GOLDMAN, CPA

TIP #1
BEGIN WITH "YES"

Answering every question with "yes" may seem over-promising, or even outright crazy, but there is a reason behind the philosophy of trying to start every answer you give with a "yes."

When someone asks you if you can accomplish a task if you do the best you can to answer their question with "yes," it makes the requester feel as if you are at least trying to help meet their need.

For example, a team member asks you, "Will we be able to complete the report by Friday?"

You could respond automatically with, "*No*, not unless we revise the requirements and don't include all the supporting documentation we originally planned on including."

Or, you can start your answer with "yes."

"*Yes*, we can complete the report by Friday. The supporting documentation may not be as extensive as we planned on, but we can complete the report."

If you were the person asking the question, which answer would make you feel better: the answer that starts with "no," or the answer that starts with "yes"? Think about it for just a second.

You may feel neither answer is ideal, but if you are like most people, human nature leads us to feel better when we know there is at least a chance of a positive outcome. From a career perspective, the more positive-natured and solutions-oriented you can be, the more your coworkers will perceive you in a favorable light, which will lead to a happier, more successful career.

Try starting all of your responses with "yes" for a while and see what happens. It takes some practice, but I'm sure you will begin to see favorable results in the way others receive you.

TIP #2
LEARN TO CONNECT WITH PEOPLE . . .
ALL PEOPLE

As accounting professionals, our careers may start based on our technical skills; however, our relationship skills determine our ability to move forward. Whether we are talking about the ability to manage a team of subordinates, efficiently work across an organization with peers, or communicate results to our boss, it's the strength and quality of our relationships that impact the effectiveness of our communication and ultimately our career progression.

There are several actions you can take in your career to strengthen your relationship-building and communication skills. Some of those actions may include:

- Networking within professional associations

- Volunteering for special projects in your organization

- Volunteering for charitable projects in your community

- Taking any classes your company may offer in the area of communication and relationship-building

- Reading books outside of work to increase your people-skills

- Listening to audio books and podcasts related to communication

- Participating in professional development groups such as Toastmasters

- Genuinely making an effort to get to know others within your organization

Although many people tend to think of accounting as a numbers-driven profession, it indeed is a people-oriented profession. There may be a few accounting roles that do not involve working with others, but that is rare in today's business climate. Learning to communicate effectively with our peers, subordinates, and supervisors is crucial to our future advancement potential.

TIP #3
CULTIVATE THE RELATIONSHIP BETWEEN YOUR SUPERVISOR AND YOURSELF

One of the leading causes, *if not the leading cause*, for an individual leaving their job, has long been the lack of a quality relationship with their supervisor. It doesn't matter if the job ends due to termination, resignation, layoff, or any other possible reason—the quality of the relationship with the manager is almost always a factor.

Your relationship with your boss is like any other relationship in your life: it takes work to cultivate and maintain. Just as you want and expect your boss to show genuine interest in your needs, your boss also wants to know that you care about his or her needs as well. While we tend not to want to get too personal in today's workplace, it does pay off to be able to relate to your coworkers on somewhat of a personal level.

If you notice your boss isn't in a good mood, or that something is bothering them, ask about it! See if there is something you can do to help. It can be lonely at the top. Perhaps they need to talk. Or maybe they need help with a project in the workplace, and they are looking for someone to step up. Either way, it goes a long way toward building the relationship to offer to help in whatever way you can.

It's human nature to appreciate it when others show us they care. Yes, we have to draw some lines and boundaries, but just because your boss is your boss doesn't mean you can't be friends on some level. Don't try to build the friendship to get ahead; do it because it's the right thing to do.

TIP #4
MISUNDERSTANDING BETWEEN
YOU AND THE BOSS? ADDRESS IT!

Just like with any other relationship, misunderstandings left uncorrected between you and your boss can cause <u>serious</u> damage. Perhaps the misunderstanding is something as severe as a disagreement you regret, or maybe it is something as slight as a mis-worded email you didn't initially consider an issue.

Either way, if you notice something has changed between you and your boss, whether or not you know exactly what happened, have a conversation and ask. It's better to bring an issue or misunderstanding out in the open early before it has time to fester and grow into a rift in the relationship.

If you have an idea of what the issue may be and are willing to take responsibility to find a solution, then sincerely apologize for the misunderstanding. We all can tell when an apology is offered simply because the other person believes it is expected, versus genuinely being apologetic. A sincere apology is always appreciated, even if it takes a little time to process.

Don't linger on the issue. Once you've offered an apology, lingering on the issue can cause more misunderstanding to occur as we search for words to fill the space. It's best to say what needs to be said, smile, and move on.

What if you don't know what the issue is, but you feel an awkwardness in your interactions? It may seem obvious, but just ask if something is bothering the other person. Perhaps something you did or did not do has caused them some concern.

Once again, it's best to bring any issues out in the open rather than to let them fester. A misunderstanding may go away after verbalizing the problem. Perhaps they need to get what is bothering them off their chest, and it won't be a long-term issue. Either way, it's best to bring up any concerns that may be damaging communication and the quality of the relationship before the situation grows into more of an issue than it needs to be.

TIP #5
YES, MENTORS ARE IMPORTANT

Motivational speaker, Jim Rohn said, "You're the average of the five people you spend the most time with." We often don't have a choice of who we spend the most time with—our coworkers, family members, and so on. However, we do have somewhat of a choice on who we allow to influence us. It is 100% our choice who to listen to, who to seek out, and where we spend quality time.

While you may have heard the term a "self-made-man" or "self-made-woman," in reality, no such people exist— no matter how glamorous it sounds. No one achieves any level of success in a vacuum. We all have some help or favor along the way. We will frequently meet mentors, or influencers, due to forces beyond our control such as a company process or divine intervention. Watch and listen to the people around you. Who is on your life path that can help you move forward?

To paraphrase a famous proverb, "Plans fail when there is a lack of advisors." You will likely find that having several mentors or influencers in your life makes more sense than having just one. Yes, we can learn a lot from one helpful individual, but no one can be everything you need. Though there are areas where you can learn from each person, there are also areas in each person that are lacking. Having several mentors to learn from along the way will help you grow in all aspects of your life. If you have only one mentor, you may only learn about the area where they are thriving.

Look around for individuals who not only have more career experience but also have more life experience than you do. Choose mentors who exhibit both the professional characteristics AND the personal characteristics you are looking to build. Both sides are equally important.

It does no good to learn from a person and emulate their career, only to find their personal life is somehow lacking in an area you consider important. It's critical to consider both career and personal success when choosing who to learn from, as a person's character will impact the choices they make in their career. Sometimes we won't be able to find the perfectly balanced mentor, as hard as we may try. In that case, we must have a strong enough sense of our character and values to draw clear boundaries concerning what we will glean from a mentor when we notice red flags.

If we can't find a person to learn directly from, there are always other resources such as books, educational classes, and podcasts, we can learn from in seasons where we don't have access to a live mentor. No matter who is in our lives, we can always choose to learn, grow, and become better both personally and professionally. Connecting to others who are further down the path will propel our endeavors.

TIP #6
CONNECTING ISN'T ENOUGH . . .
YOU HAVE TO STAY CONNECTED

It's relatively common to become involved in professional organizations and networking when we are considering a job change, particularly when we are actively searching for a new opportunity. Unfortunately, it's just as common for us to draw back or even let go of relationships we worked so hard to build after we have secured a new opportunity or stopped searching for whatever reason. Over time, as we focus in on our new job, we often naturally stop attending association mixers, volunteer events, and the occasional lunch with friends in our profession. In the process, we lose out on relationships.

There are many benefits to remaining active in networking and in a professional organization other than just looking for job opportunities. By staying connected with other professionals both inside and outside your profession, you nurture intellectual well-roundedness and keep up with the trends influencing business. By staying connected, you have an active peer group you can turn to for support if you need to discuss professional issues or ethical dilemmas.

I may be stating the obvious, but, when you stay connected, new career opportunities are likely to find you without you having to work so hard to find them. When you remain connected in your profession people notice you and view you as more of an expert in your field. People seek out experts who stay connected in their profession. They rarely have to look hard for new opportunities. Stay connected even when you're not looking for a new job, and you will be less likely ever to have to look for a new opportunity again. The opportunities will come to you.

TIP #7
ALWAYS TAKE THE HIGH ROAD AND NEVER BURN A BRIDGE

I guess you could make the argument that taking the high road doesn't always pay off in the short-term, but I think we all know that choosing the proverbial high road, or doing the right thing, pays off in the long-run. It may cost us time, money, or other things now, but we always feel better about ourselves and our actions later on—and that's not even considering other benefits.

Generally, when we find it difficult to make the right choice we are often overemphasizing the immediate consequences such as losing money, time, or "face." We may also have another person influencing or attempting to influence us to make the wrong choice. If you find yourself in one of these situations, remove yourself from outside influences, at least temporarily, and focus on how the long-term consequences of your actions may play out.

Think about one year from now, two years from now, or even ten years from now. How will you feel about the situation and your actions at that point? Looking at the potential future outcomes is generally the best gauge of how you should act now. If you will be happier with your choices in the future, it is worth whatever short-term consequence or loss is required now.

Also, never underestimate the potential long-term losses that come from burning a bridge and damaging a relationship. No doubt about it, burning a bridge is always, 100 percent of the time, a detrimental idea. We run across the same people in life and our careers more frequently than we usually anticipate. Even putting the value of doing the right thing aside, you never know when you will run across the same person again, or someone they know or influence.

TIP #8
BUILD BRIDGES TOO!

The managing partner of a very successful CPA firm once told me that one of the secrets to his success was "building bridges, and you do that with people."

I think the idea of building bridges seems simple enough to most of us. When someone refers to building a bridge, we naturally think about being nice and considerate of the people around us. I'm not as confident that we think about bridge building as an ongoing process. I would like to challenge us to think more deeply into the concept.

It's not only one bridge that we need to build, but many bridges. We not only need to build, but we need to maintain the bridges we build as well. We don't build bridges just to use them one time; we build them for multiple uses, and to reach various destinations.

Bridges are relationships. We can't do anything well without healthy relationships supporting us. We need to build and maintain healthy relationships in our lives.

I do have a caveat, though. When we talk about the impact of healthy interpersonal relationships on a career, it is easy to slip into the thought of "using people" to go where you want to go. Please don't misunderstand. I in no way mean you should use relationships to get ahead—that is just pure manipulation.

Instead, the point I'm making is quite the contrary. You can't expect to do well without having consideration for the people around you. If you always take the needs of others into account and even put them ahead of your own, you find that your needs tend to be taken care of without much worry.

TIP #9
SPEAK THE TRUTH . . . TACTFULLY

I'm taking a risk putting the following estimation in writing, but I think it is safe to say that the majority (51+ percent) of people in the accounting profession lean toward being anti-confrontational. There are certainly those in the industry that appreciate an active discussion, but there are also many that prefer a more peaceful environment. Being a peace-loving person is a trait that can, unfortunately, occasionally work to our detriment.

Truth is valued in the business world, particularly by owners and executive managers—at least the good ones. While it's important to be tactful about potentially sensitive issues, it's equally essential to discuss problems. The most disappointing situation a manager or owner can face is to have something go wrong, only to find out a team member saw the issue in advance and didn't speak up for fear of upsetting someone.

Managers have to make sure they create an environment where feedback is welcome, but as team members, we also need to be willing to push outside of our comfort zone and speak up when we notice something we need to address. We do no good by staying quiet to save someone's feelings in the short-term, only to see a more significant issue arise later on that we could have prevented. By not speaking up, we become part of the problem when we could have been part of the solution instead.

If you notice something that needs to be addressed, even if no one else notices, speak up. Even if it is a misunderstanding on your part, it's extremely rare that the misunderstanding will have long-term negative consequences for you. Instead, people will appreciate that you cared enough to address your concerns. Alternatively, if the issue is major and you were the one to point it out, then you become the person that was willing to step up and save the day. "Hero" may be too strong a word, but you never know . . .

TIP #10
BE PRESENT WITH THE PEOPLE YOU'RE PRESENTLY WITH

One of the best relationship-building habits you can develop is to be present with the individuals you are presently with at any particular moment. Pay attention to what they are saying. Be aware of how they are saying it. Take note of what they don't say. Really listen without thinking of how you will respond or what you have to do afterward. You've likely heard this before, but one of the most frequent mistakes human beings make is listening to respond instead of listening to understand.

We live in a world of constant bombardment. The people around us, our environment, advertising, the internet, and many other distractions compete for our attention—not to mention we have to fight against our own stray thoughts! Being present with the individuals you are presently with is a valuable gift that you alone have the power to give to them.

It's so rare these days for us to have someone's undivided attention. We all appreciate when someone is really paying attention to what we are saying. If you practice staying mentally and emotionally present with the people you are with, it will set you apart as a good listener, a good leader, and even as a good friend.

TIP #11
FIND A CAREER ADVISOR—DON'T JUST RELY ON YOUR SIGNIFICANT OTHER

We all need an outside trusted career advisor, or advisors, to bounce thoughts off of as we contemplate which direction to take next. Whether we are considering a job change, strategizing on how to ask for a promotion, or simply navigating a touchy situation at work, it always helps to have a fresh perspective from someone you can trust.

While a relationship with a significant other is frequently and appropriately the most trusting relationship you may have, it's generally difficult for the person closest to you to give unbiased feedback on your career situation because they are too emotionally involved to stay neutral. It's best if your career-strategy mentor is someone you respect, but not someone you are extremely close to. In fact, it's generally best if it's someone you don't even work with, as their situation may be too closely tied to yours as well.

Proactively asking for advice is not the only key to success; the person you ask help of is also important. That person may be someone you consider to be your mentor, or possibly not, depending on the nature of your relationship. The term "mentor" means different things to different people. When choosing a person to confide in, consider former bosses, professionals you have met through other networks, former coworkers, peers from college, or any other professional you can trust to give you confidential and honest feedback.

TIP #12
NETWORK <u>WITHIN</u> YOUR ORGANIZATION

I never thought of getting to know the people within your own company as "networking" until I was speaking with an executive at a major employer that referred to it that way. We were talking about the advice he would give young professionals on how to be successful. To paraphrase, he said, "Be sure to 'network' within your organization as well."

We all know it is essential to network with outside professionals, but I think it is safe to say that when we think of networking, we tend to think of participating in professional organizations, volunteering, or involvement in civic organizations as a way to meet people. Many of us don't think about networking in terms of being acquainted with others within our own company; but if we think about it, networking within our organization is much more likely to benefit us career-wise.

Networking within our organization not only makes us more well-known and therefore noticed when it comes to advancement opportunities, but it can also make our daily jobs more manageable because we have connections within the company. In a nutshell, while it's important to network with professionals outside of your organization, you can't neglect your current organization in the process. It's just as important, and possibly more so, to get to know your internal colleagues as it is to meet outside professionals.

TIP #13
ALWAYS RESPOND TO EMAILS, VOICEMAILS, AND TEXTS

Develop the habit of acknowledging every message you receive. You may not always have an immediate answer to the request but communicating <u>receipt</u> and that you will be in touch goes a long way. Responding with something as basic as, "Thank you. I will get back with you shortly," is enough to give you time to work on a proper response.

I do not recommend using an auto-responder for daily communication though. An automatic reply serves a valuable purpose when you're out of the office, but otherwise, it does not give the recipient assurance you saw their message. In fact, it can leave a person feeling just as frustrated as not receiving any acknowledgment at all.

When a sender does not receive a response, it often leaves them wondering what happened and assuming the worst. You may not see their message as urgent, but the *sender is* important. Responding in a way that lets the sender know you have seen their message at least lets them know you have heard them. It takes away any uncertainty that you may not care, may not agree with, or simply may not have received their message.

As great as technology is, it is not always dependable. Even using a reliable delivery system doesn't guarantee a message was successfully received, read, or even noticed. Email systems have multiple spam filters that sometimes catch non-spam messages; voicemail systems can falter; a message may be accidentally deleted or syncing between devices might fail to update. Though we know technology may have hiccuped, a technical problem isn't usually our first automatic thought about why we didn't receive a response to a message we sent. Too often, our go-to assumption is much more negative and personal. We can proactively guard our reputations against technology mishaps by setting the positive precedent of consistently responding.

When we develop the habit of responding to all messages, we teach others that we care, and what to expect from us concerning communication. If we have interacted quickly through messaging systems in the past and then suddenly fail to acknowledge one message, it will likely result in the sender giving us the benefit of the doubt and reaching out again. They will be less likely to assume the worst.

TIP #14
LEARN TO PROBLEM-SOLVE

People hire people to accomplish tasks. Finding a solution is not the only valuable asset you can provide as an employee, *attempting* to find solutions is also a valuable trait—particularly when you are new on the job. The more a supervisor has to guide you through a process, or even work with you for the duration of a project, the less valuable you are. Of course, we should ask for help or clarification when it is needed, but it's best to first step back and think about a solution to the problem before immediately jumping to ask for assistance.

A good supervisor will want to help you when needed, but if they truly are a good supervisor then above that, they will want you to grow. Thinking through issues yourself is a part of the growth process. Even if you ultimately don't come to a solution on your own, the mere study of the situation has a benefit.

Always study the problem a little yourself before asking for help, but don't consider it for too long! Step back and review the situation. Think through the cause of the issue and the options you have to solve the problem. If you can't come up with a final solution, do you have an idea on how to prevent the issue in the future? Knowing about the problem in and of itself is a win! You will at least have a much better understanding of the problem and learn more when you do request assistance from your boss.

TIP #15
EMBRACE CHANGE

Most career paths end up dramatically different than we initially plan. Many things can happen. We may realize we don't enjoy what we thought we would enjoy. Maybe a better opportunity than we ever anticipated comes around, and we decide to go a new direction.

It's important to be open to change and not too regimented about how our careers "should" go. It's important to have a plan to start with; we need initial direction. It's just as important though to adapt along the way to the opportunities and challenges that may come along.

Going through college, I just knew I was going to work in public accounting and then become a partner in a firm. I even had a typical backup plan to become a Controller or CFO in a large company if the right opportunity came available along the way. Neither of my ideas came to fruition.

Very early in my career, I had the opportunity to serve the accounting community, instead of working within it. It fit my needs at the time, so I decided to give it a shot. Little did I know that the opportunities would work together over the years to create a career path I thoroughly enjoy. I love working in the employment field with accountants! Sure, it wasn't my "master plan," but it worked out even better for my personality. You never know what opportunities will come your way. Be open to, and embrace, change.

TIP #16
LEARN TO LOVE LEARNING

Most of us graduate college with at least the subconscious thought, if not verbalizing the bold statement, that we are "done" studying for a while. The feeling can be even more intense after we go through the rigorous preparation to pass a certification exam.

The fact is, we never stop learning; however, our process of learning transitions. We move from studying theoretical classroom knowledge to picking up daily on-the-job practical experience that we are expected to put to use immediately.

Teaching yourself to enjoy learning is an important trait if you want to have a progressively successful career. In fact, it's related to embracing change as well. If you enjoy learning new things, then you are more likely to positively respond when presented with new projects or initiatives at work because you will naturally view them as opportunities to learn more.

Learning doesn't stop with college or certification. It is a career-long endeavor that the smartest among us teach ourselves to appreciate. Learn to love learning!

TIP #17
BE GRACIOUS AND APPRECIATIVE

Learning always to be gracious and appreciative of anything we receive is an attitude we should all strive to cultivate. No one likes an unappreciative individual, no matter how successful they are. A lack of appreciation and grace comes across as arrogance.

We all strive to be the best we can be. Many in our society embrace the idea of being a "self-made" man or woman. If you have a driven, accomplishment-oriented personality, it is easy to drift into having a little too much pride. The truth is none of us achieve any level of success without assistance along the way.

Always remember the people that helped you get where you are. Remember the people that help you to achieve what you achieve every day. Remember other people work very hard and are just as talented as you are, but have had different circumstances in their lives that have possibly led them not to be quite as fortunate as you are.

No matter how hard we work—and we should work hard—we need to be appreciative and gracious regarding the life we have. If you build a courteous attitude within yourself, you will find the payoff is a life of greater contentment and happiness, no matter where you are at on your career journey.

TIP #18
OWN YOUR MISTAKES

A common theme that has emerged during many of our podcast interviews with successful accountants is: "Own your mistakes." The comment implies the inevitable realization that we will all make mistakes at some point. It's an interesting observation given that in general, the world seems a little less forgiving of accounting mistakes since they typically involve money.

The reality is, mistakes do happen—no matter what profession you work in. Thankfully we work in a field where, although inconvenient, there are usually not dire consequences to our mistakes, particularly if we recognize and correct them early.

When you admit you've made a mistake, most people will forgive quickly. On the other hand, many people tend to remember a situation longer when you fail to admit a mistake, and the situation grows worse. For many, it is unforgivable, or at least hard-to-forgive, situations when a person refuses to take responsibility for their mistakes.

When you notice you have made a mistake of some type, whether large or small, immediately address it. Admit to and own the situation. Everyone makes mistakes, and most of us realize that. Owning your mistakes early will not only prevent further damage, but it will also earn other's respect.

TIP #19
TABLE STAKES ARE TABLE STAKES, BUT THEY ARE ONLY TABLE STAKES

For those not familiar with the gambling term, "table stakes" are the costs of what it takes to get into a game—the minimum bet if you will. Technical knowledge is the "table stakes" of the accounting world. I started to think about technical knowledge in this way after interviewing a partner from a national accounting firm.

Obviously, it's imperative to know what you are doing as an accountant from a technical perspective. It's also important for others to trust that you know what you are doing. Even though good grades and an understanding of technical concepts are essential, they indeed are just the "table stakes," or the minimal requirements, for an accounting job. As your career starts, you will quickly realize that other skills, such as communication and leadership, become just as important, and even more important, than your technical knowledge.

As your career progresses, your ability to move up and to be successful in your role will depend much more upon "soft skills" rather than technical skills. If you increase your leadership ability, you will likely end up supervising people that handle the technical aspects of the job, while you oversee their work. Management—or the oversight of work—requires more soft skills than technical skills.

Still, don't forgo doing well in your technical studies. Just make sure you are developing your communication and leadership along with increasing your knowledge. Your older self will thank you for it later!

TIP #20
SHOW UP

"Showing up is half the battle."

There is truth in that statement. Merely being dependable to show up as expected, when expected, and prepared for whatever you were supposed to be prepared for, goes a long way toward your success. Whether it is consistently showing up for work, arriving on time for client appointments, or even volunteering to help out a friend or colleague, dependability is a key characteristic of leadership.

Showing up when expected is not just a time or schedule issue, but an issue of respect. By showing up on time, you show you respect the individual or individuals with whom you are meeting. Conversely, showing up late or unprepared is often seen as a sign that you don't appreciate the person you were meeting, or at least their time, enough to plan.

Everyone is busy these days, so when we make an effort to show up on time, we communicate our respect. The person you are meeting with knows you are busy; they are busy too. It is disappointing when we commit our time and effort to being available when the other party doesn't show up on time or isn't prepared.

Being dependable is an essential characteristic of the accounting field, but unfortunately, it isn't a universal trait. Merely showing up as expected is the first step in differentiating yourself in any situation.

TIP #21
LEARN MICROSOFT EXCEL VERY WELL

Practice,
Practice
and more
Practice
and you will
Excel!!

Yes, I know . . . someday, you will have "people" to do your spreadsheets. Until then though, it is a smart move to learn as much about Excel as you can. Take an online tutorial, practice what you learn, and pay attention when you are around a more advanced user.

In college, your priority is learning technical accounting skills. Even if you used Excel for every school assignment, your skills would still need some work and advancement once you graduate to stay on par with more experienced coworkers. Excel itself will also continue to update, and it will be necessary to continue to learn new ways of using the software.

Even though accounting systems continuously change, the need for spreadsheet skills is likely never to go away. With any structured accounting system comes limitations to how much and how quickly you can customize it. With Excel being by far the leading spreadsheet software, it makes sense to become an advanced user.

And, even when you do have "people" to do this work for you, you will likely find that employers prefer team members that are "hands-on," meaning that you have the skills to do some of the work yourself if necessary. Spreadsheet software skills will continue to be an asset throughout your career.

TIP #22
DEVELOP ANALYTICAL SKILLS

As accounting software becomes more and more advanced, our ability as accountants to simply record transactions accurately becomes less valuable. Employers and clients will look to us more for the analysis of the information, not just for the data itself. The expectation for accountants to provide analysis began years ago and continues to grow in prominence. Train yourself to look past the numbers to discover what the numbers mean. The numbers should tell you something, not just reflect a record of transactions.

How can we develop analytical skills? Primarily, it is something we have to practice intentionally. As you prepare reports, ask yourself: What is the report communicating? Does it look correct? What does the report show? What does it mean for the future of the business? What are some areas for improvement?

If you train yourself to think more analytically, versus just reviewing for accuracy, you will create a much more valuable skill set in the long run. Your ability to analyze and communicate data will serve you well as your career progresses.

TIP #23
GROW YOUR SYSTEMS AND OPERATIONS KNOWLEDGE

We've talked a lot about the importance of people skills. If you had to choose any one thing to develop outside of technical accounting skills, people skills would be the most important area to work on. Communication, leadership, empathy, and general relationship building skills are the most important areas to develop if you want to continue to grow your career. There are two other areas—outside of technical expertise and people skills—that you should work on as well though: systems and operations knowledge.

By systems, I mean both the software-specific sense of the word and the general sense of the word. The more diverse and up-to-date your computer system experience is, the more valuable you will be to both your current employer and any future employer you may choose to work with. Knowing how to work in a variety of systems makes job advancement easier, but it also enables you to adapt to new systems much easier as well.

Operations is also an important growth area. The more you understand how a business operates in the overall sense, the more valuable you will be as an advisor in that business. Having a skill set and mindset of operations will make you exponentially more valuable. The more knowledgeable and talented you are concerning the operations of a company—how they make a profit—the better a general business advisor you become.

If you think about it, when you understand not just the finance or accounting side of a business, but also the people, systems, and operations sides, you become well-rounded in all the aspects of running the business, and that is a great position to be in.

TIP #24
STAY CURIOUS AND ASK QUESTIONS

As our careers move forward, we become responsible for finding and choosing our own educational opportunities. In college, we follow a specific plan, but after college, other than a few continuing education courses our employers may require, we are left to choose how we grow and in which direction we develop, if any.

One way to continue to learn is to stay curious and ask questions. For the most part, people appreciate questions in the workplace because it shows you care and are interested in what is going on. You need to make sure the questions you ask aren't self-serving, but instead show an interest in the situation at hand—your company, coworkers, and the problems that need to be solved. Staying curious is one of the best ways to find opportunities for continued growth.

An accounting executive who specialized in change management once told me that early in his career he found himself curious about why things were happening the way they were happening. He was interested not just at the superficial level, but at a deeper solutions-oriented level. Consequently, he became the go-to person to head-up situations when the solution involved a high level of organizational change.

His curiosity worked well for him. He held positions such as the Vice President of Finance, the Executive Vice President, and eventually became the President of a company. Staying curious and wanting to continue to learn effectively fueled his career. Don't be afraid to ask questions. It pays off.

TIP #25
AS SOON AS YOU THINK YOU KNOW EVERYTHING, YOU BECOME OBSOLETE

We've referenced the benefits of continuous learning a few times, but we haven't talked about the other side of the topic—the danger in not continuing to learn. Sure, some of the basics of accounting don't change; however, it's just the very basics that don't change. For example, I suspect a debit will still be a debit twenty years from now. Everything else changes though, and change happens even more quickly the more time that goes by.

Accounting law and procedures update. Prevalent technology in the workplace changes. Leadership styles that work well with some generations end up working poorly with other generations.

If you don't continue to learn and develop over time, you will find yourself left behind in the workplace. If you don't continue to progress, your skills will be outdated. Eventually, you will see that your once-valued skills have become irrelevant, obsolete, or are now delegated to electronics.

At any point in your career, telling yourself that you have learned everything you need to know is a dangerous attitude to have. None of us have "arrived." Thinking that we know it all only leads to one thing: obsolescence.

TIP #26
"COMFORT IS THE ENEMY
OF ACHIEVEMENT"

As far as I have been able to research, the above quote is credited to Farrah Gray, the author of several books. I first heard it from a newly certified CPA though as he described what it takes to achieve certification.

As much as I would like to say differently, it requires sacrifice to study for and pass a certification exam such as the CPA, CMA, CIA, etc. By the time we start to prepare for such an exam, our life is well underway. We have already graduated or are just about to graduate from college. Most people are already working full-time, and many have significant social and family commitments. "Squeezing in" study time just isn't possible without "lessening" something else for a while.

Some people decide to work part-time as they prepare for a major exam, but that option isn't practical for most. Others try to squeeze in brief study sessions here and there, but that generally isn't effective. Most people will need to sacrifice social activities and maybe even some family weekend time to pass their exams. I know that was the case for me personally at least.

The idea that "comfort is the enemy of achievement" very much applies to earning a certification. Don't feel bad if you feel as if you are missing out on life; your study time is temporary. Your investment and sacrifice will pay off later, not just financially, but in other ways as well.

TIP #27
NEVER LET GO OF A CERTIFICATION

No matter what you feel your long-term plans may be, never let go of certification unless you intend to retire fully, and even then many people choose to keep their certifications active into retirement! Certifications take considerable effort to acquire—sometimes literal blood, sweat, and tears, or at least sweat and tears. Although there are costs to maintaining a certification, reinstating after a lapse is much more substantial in terms of both time and money.

I've met many people that let a certification lapse and realized, later on, they would be better off if they still had it. I have never, ever, ever met anyone that told me they let their certification lapse and they were happy they did. I'm sure there is someone out there somewhere that has done so, but I have yet to meet them.

Before you decide to let a certification go, consider other options first. Perhaps pursuing less expensive continuing education would help. Or maybe doing some work on the side to cover the costs of maintaining the certification would make sense. In some parts of the country, you can select a type of inactive status that minimizes the time and monetary investment of maintaining your certification.

If at all possible, don't let your certification go. The likelihood that later in life you would have benefited from keeping it active is too great. Certification is a wonderful achievement, and you worked very hard to accomplish it. It is worth maintaining.

TIP #28
CERTIFICATIONS PAY LIKE AN ANNUITY

Many, if not most of us, have seen the charts showing how much of a difference it makes if you start saving for retirement early in life versus later on in your career. If you think about it, attaining certification is similar. The sooner you can attain a certification such as the CPA, CMA, or one of the others, the sooner it begins to pay off.

The sooner you have a certification, the sooner you qualify for higher-level positions, and the sooner you will receive a raise in your current role. Even if you are self-employed or a consultant, you are likely to be able to charge more for your services if you hold a certification.

The earlier you attain certification and take advantage of the opportunities it brings you, the more the benefits will compound over time. Waiting several years to pursue certification is sort of like putting off saving until later in life. You will miss out on the compound interest it earns over time. Since pay increases are frequently based on a level of qualification or a percentage above current earnings, that same compounding principal applies here as well.

The sooner you are certified, the sooner compounding starts. Certifications really do pay off much like an annuity. That being said, it is never too late to begin pursuing certification—just like it's never too late to start saving for the future.

TIP #29
LEARN ABOUT BUSINESS,
NOT JUST ABOUT ACCOUNTING

The more you can learn about all aspects of business, the more it will benefit your overall career. Whether you work for an individual company, an accounting firm, or are self-employed, more knowledge equals more value. Teach yourself to be genuinely interested in the overall business operations of your employer or clients, as the case may be. Not only will your knowledge pay off, but it will also result in a much more interesting career.

If you work in an organization that doesn't give you the opportunity to learn more about other areas of the business, you can still take steps to further your knowledge. Reading books or listening to audio-books is a great way to stretch your business acumen outside of daily accounting tasks. Meeting professionals that work in other areas is also a great way to gain insight into how general business functions, even if the other person doesn't work for your employer.

Accountants have a strong background for learning other areas of business. We understand what affects cash flow and have an understanding of business basics because it is a part of our bachelor's degree. The more you learn about tangent areas, the more valuable an advisor you become to your clients or your employer.

TIP #30
LEARN TO STAY HUMBLE . . .
MOST OF THE TIME

Overall, accountants tend to be more humble than boastful, at least on average. It may sound counterintuitive, but although humility is a generally positive trait, there are times when it doesn't serve us well. While humility works very well in the business world on a daily basis, there are circumstances when we need to step out and be a little more forward about our talent and worth.

When it comes time to discuss your compensation level or performance, it's vital to point out your achievements tactfully. Of course, it is not appropriate to "toot your own horn" daily, but it is appropriate to do so somewhat as your employer evaluates financial compensation.

Many people don't want to overstep or appear conceited, even when it comes to discussing their compensation. When talking about your salary though, it's not a time to downplay your accomplishments. Be honest with yourself about your value, and make sure you adequately express your worth.

TIP #31
WISH OUT LOUD

As I interviewed a director from one of the national accounting firms, I asked her to identify the keys to her career success. That's when she mentioned that she had made a habit of "wishing out loud." I had never heard anyone attribute success to "wishing." The concept is simple enough though, and it works well when coupled with a humble attitude.

The idea of wishing aloud is that instead of directly asking for a position or opportunity, or continually trying to work your way up, you mention what you hope for in the course of normal conversation. For example, if you're talking to someone who works in an area that you would like to work in, say, "Wow. I wish I had the chance to do something like this."

You have to express your wishes to people that have the power to make your dream come true, even if only in the future. If you are going to verbalize your desire, do it around people that influence that area. Otherwise, it may not go much further than being a wish!

Wishing aloud is an interesting tactic, and although it may seem a tad sneaky, if it's done genuinely then it isn't anything more than honesty. Try harnessing the power of "wishing out loud" to find the long-term opportunities you desire. You are likely to be pleasantly surprised when your wish comes true.

TIP #32
YOU WILL BE KNOWN FOR SOMETHING
. . . LIKE IT OR NOT

You may think of "personal branding" as something that only marketing or sales-related professionals have to think about, but it applies to all professions. Whether you like it or not, you will become known for something or possibly even many things.

Take time to think about what you want to be known for, or in other words the impression you want to leave people with after they interact with you. Work on how to cultivate making a positive impression, and work on developing your desired character traits. It's important to be genuine, but most of us need a little internal buffer.

You can't control the fact that people will draw conclusions about you based on what they see, hear, and how you treat them, but you can work to become the person that you genuinely want to be. Take the time to develop the "you" that you wish to become. Take control of your brand.

TIP #33
DO THE RIGHT THING
WHEN NO ONE IS WATCHING

Yes, I know. This tip is so cliché; however, it's still very true. As accountants, we are expected to maintain the highest level of integrity. Historically accountants rank among the most-trusted professionals in our society. It sounds simple, but doing the right thing often requires courage, strength, and sacrifice.

Sometimes there is an initial pain associated with making the right choice, particularly if someone else wants you to do the wrong thing. At times, there may be no material benefit to acting with integrity. You may even experience loss associated with your choice. No matter how it may feel at the moment, making the ethical decision always feels better in the long-run, not to mention it's the moral thing to do.

As accountants, we come across many situations in our careers where we have the opportunity to make bad decisions that seemingly won't hurt anyone. Even if we think our choice will not affect others, making the wrong choice often does hurt other people. We just don't realize the potential consequences at the moment. At a minimum we will hurt ourselves by compromising our integrity, which can result in regret and take years to overcome.

Always do the right thing, regardless of whether anyone will notice it or not. Do the right thing, even if it hurts. To continue with the cliché, do the right thing—it's the right thing to do.

TIP #34
GIVE BACK

Through my years of speaking with successful accounting professionals, one thing I've learned is that giving back is a key to success. Giving to those in need, or simply giving to the community in general, keeps us humble. It makes us realize how truly blessed we are.

It's very possible you may be thinking, "I don't have much, so what can I give?" Maybe you are just starting your career, or perhaps you are still a college student trying to pay for next semester. Maybe you won't even be able to attend college next year due to financial constraints.

You do not necessarily have to give financially to give back. It may be that you provide a listening ear. Everyone needs someone to listen to them. Many of us are in need of someone to simply care for us, even more so than we are in need of financial help.

The principle of giving is not dependent on how much or how little you have. There is always someone somewhere that has less than you do and could use help. As you continue to grow in your career, always remember to make time for charitable activities. Be a blessing to others. Be a giver.

TIP #35
DON'T JUST WORK . . . GET INVOLVED

We've talked about giving back in the general sense, but there is also value in giving back specifically to your profession. Most professional associations need volunteers. Giving your time and talent to your profession provides resources for others to grow.

Your involvement also provides an opportunity for you to grow as well. You will grow personally, and you will learn skills and gain abilities you may not learn on the job. Other professionals will appreciate you donating your time for the betterment of all of us. You will become a better person and a better professional.

The personal growth benefits I mentioned don't even start to touch on the benefits of career networking that come through volunteering. Through giving your time to a professional organization, you will meet people you otherwise wouldn't meet. You may meet your next boss, your next new hire, or your next coworker through your efforts. In the long run, you will likely receive more out of volunteering than you give.

Regardless of whether or not any networking value comes out of your activity, give of your time and talent to your profession. It will pay off for all of us in the long-run. Oh, and thank you. ☺

TIP #36
FOR THE MOST PART, BE PREDICTABLE

I know being predictable isn't exactly a popular concept these days. We all want to be different, unique, and to stand out. But, it's important to remember when it comes to our professional lives, people like predictable accountants.

Whether you are self-employed or working for a corporation, reporting to clients or reporting to a boss, people appreciate knowing the work will be done as expected, and when expected. When people are counting on us, they like predictability. Yes, we can be a little unique, but when performing services, be predictable.

Does being predictable mean you have to be exactly like everyone else or even fit the typical accountant stereotype? No, it does not! But in general, people don't like surprises from their accountants; they want predictability. They don't like us to surprise them with a missed deadline, or a higher than expected tax liability. They love us to be predictably responsible in our actions. They want to know they can trust us.

TIP #37
MONEY ISN'T EVERYTHING, UNLESS IT'S FIDUCIARY MONEY!

General Ledger					
Account: Cash					
Date	Description	ref#	Debit	Credit	Balance
4/12	Deposit	J1	$200.00	$0.00	$3200.00
4/14	Payment Vase Sale	J1	$0.00	$400.00	$2800.00

It's quite an ironic concept for accountants, but one way or another we all eventually learn the timeless truth that "money isn't everything." Even though money isn't everything, it's incredible how concerned people can become when they think we've made a mistake with their money! ☺ I'm being tongue-in-cheek on this topic, but how we treat money really is a two-fold issue as accountants.

Every day, we make decisions about how to spend our time. We make trade-offs between work and personal time. We need to make our daily decisions with balance in mind. It's important for us to remember that money really is not everything.

On the other hand, when we are handling other people's money under a fiduciary duty, or making decisions that affect someone else's profit or loss, we need to give the responsibility a higher level of importance. Making our fiduciary responsibility a priority generally involves an increased level of communication. It also typically involves paying more attention to pennies than we may in our own personal finances.

To sum it up, don't let money rule your life, but if it is someone else's money then give it more care than you would your own.

TIP #38
DON'T LET MISTAKES PARALYZE YOU

Mistakes are natural, and we should expect to make them occasionally. But, given that we work with information that either directly or indirectly affects other's livelihoods, sometimes our mistakes as accountants are met with less grace than in other fields.

As I previously pointed out, it's essential to own up to it immediately when you make a mistake. Do your best to fix the situation and communicate. It's also important not to let the commission of an error paralyze you or hinder you from moving forward in your career.

It's true; everyone makes mistakes whether we like it or not. What is more important is how we move forward after making a mistake; that is the real test of a professional.

TIP #39
ALWAYS BE A LITTLE
COMPETITIVE WITH YOURSELF

There are times in life when we need to slow down and take it easy. Sometimes we need to stop and survey where we have been and what we have accomplished. No matter how driven we may be, we can't always focus on rapid progression every minute of our lives.

We also can't always compare ourselves to others. In fact, if you want to make sure you are disappointed, or even depressed about your position in life, a sure way to get there is to compare yourself to others. There is always someone that either has or appears to have, a better situation than you do.

The right way to approach competition is to be competitive with yourself. Our calling in life is to be the best "us" we can be. No other comparison matters.

We all are unique, and therefore shouldn't be trying to be just like someone else. Sure, we may try to attain a particular position or goal in life, but we will never be exactly like another person. Focus instead on merely being better than you were yesterday, and you will ultimately become the person you want to become.

TIP #40
LOVE WHAT YOU DO,
OR DO SOMETHING ELSE

For the record, I'm NOT suggesting that anyone leave our accounting profession. That would be heresy! That being said, there are many jobs you can do with a background or education in accounting where you may never touch a tax return or an audit. You may even barely see the general ledger. Not that those tasks are bad or unlovable; in fact, I happened to enjoy those areas of accounting myself!

As your career develops though, if you find you don't quite enjoy what you are doing, don't be afraid to change. There is an argument that says as we gain more experience, we become more and more specialized and therefore pigeon-holed in that one area. Truthfully, over time we also become more experienced in general. With a little creativity, we can apply our experience to many other areas of accounting and find a position with responsibilities we may enjoy even more.

Every job and self-employment endeavor has good days and bad days. If you find yourself with more bad days than good, it's time to consider where else your talents may be beneficial. You will likely be more successful if you are doing something you enjoy. It does pay off to try to find something you like doing. You will be happier and even more productive in the long-run.

TIP #41
WORK TOWARD SOLUTIONS, NOT RAISES

In the broad sense, this philosophical tip will work in your overall life as well as your career. We should always strive to work toward solving problems for the greater good, not just aiming for our benefit. When you work toward solving problems by providing solutions, you work to help others, and they will notice and appreciate it. You may even find that raises and promotions come to you without you having to seek them out.

An accomplished executive once told me, "It's wise to work so diligently that your superiors have no choice but to promote you because you become so valuable [to the organization]." If you give above and beyond and still don't end up rewarded where you are, it's likely that someone from another company will seek you out. Either way, you win.

Focus on helping others and providing solutions. If you do so, you won't have to worry about gaining a promotion; it will come to you.

TIP #42
THERE'S ALWAYS A BIGGER FISH TO LEARN FROM, AND THAT'S A GOOD THING

Staying in learning mode keeps us growing, mentally alert, and young-at-heart. If you have ever met someone that has risen to a point where they don't have a mentor or someone to learn from, you likely will notice that person is dissatisfied with their situation no matter how good it may be. Sometimes they are even depressed.

As we grow in our careers, it's important always to have a mentor of sorts. Even when you hit the top, you can learn a tremendous amount from the team you supervise—if you have hired well. It's important to continue to learn from others who are more advanced in areas you would still like to grow in. But where do you find those individuals?

You may learn from a professional acquaintance as you get to know them better. You may learn from a former boss that has moved on or a business coach you hire to keep you challenged and growing. A mentor can come from just about anywhere, but you generally have to consciously look for an opportunity to connect. Mentors don't always find you.

No matter how far you go in your career, never think that there isn't anyone left to learn from. If you do find yourself feeling that way, it means you don't realize how expansive the world really is. None of us are beyond learning and growing. There is always a bigger fish to learn from; sometimes we have to search them out.

TIP #43
IF THE GRASS LOOKS GREENER ELSEWHERE, HAVE YOU WATERED YOURS?

There are times in your career when it is a good idea to look for something else, either within your company or at another organization. It could be that you've lost your passion for your current job, or maybe your relationship with your supervisor has deteriorated to the point of no return. There are also times when your career's "grass" doesn't look quite as green as others' only because you haven't watered it recently.

If you start to get the feeling that "the grass is greener" somewhere else, think about a few things before leaving.

Number one, it could be that the grass looks greener somewhere else because of how hard they work to keep it that way. Number two, it could be that your lawn isn't quite as green because you haven't worked on it much recently. Ask yourself if there is anything you can do in your current situation to make it better before deciding to move on.

Are you giving your current role 100% of your effort? Have you worked on developing your relationship with your boss? Do you feel good about the energy you are putting in overall?

There are times when a better situation exists elsewhere, but that isn't always the case. Make sure you are moving toward something better, and not just escaping something you haven't fully invested in yet.

TIP #44
DON'T COMPARE YOURSELF TO OTHERS, UNLESS YOU FIND YOURSELF PASSED UP

Comparing your position with others' positions in life is generally a recipe for unhappiness. There will always be someone somewhere that appears to have it better than you do. Whether that is reality is a different story.

Comparing yourself to others is usually a bad idea; however, if you find you are frequently passed over for promotions, not getting raises or the last to be approached about projects and other opportunities, it may be time to do a little comparison!

Does it appear that those around you are somehow putting in more effort? Is it possible that they are getting better opportunities because they are somehow better qualified? Maybe their options are coming from a relationship-driven situation, and there is something you can do to build better relationships both inside and outside of your organization as well.

It is usually a bad idea to compare yourself with others, as you rarely know their whole story or the reality of their situation, but there are times when a little comparison can help you realize areas for improvement in yourself. Guard yourself against approaching comparison with an attitude of jealousy, but instead approach it from the standpoint of wanting to be a better you.

TIP #45
KISS UP. NOT REALLY . . . BUT, YES

The term "kissing up" is definitely too strong for what I really hope to convey here. Some people consider "kissing up" to be flattery. What I'm encouraging is giving genuine compliments, *not flattery*. An honest compliment can make a big difference in even a business relationship.

We live in a management-by-exception world. What I mean is we are used to being told if something isn't working well, but most of us aren't told when something <u>is</u> working well.

A little genuine appreciation for something that is working the way it should be can go a long way. Saying "thank you" as a common courtesy is an appreciated gesture in our world today. Tell people what they are doing well. Stop for a moment every day to tell others that you appreciate their effort.

Say thank you for the most basic acts—not in a patronizing way, but genuinely. Focusing on the positive will help you build relationships. Your words of affirmation will make people feel better about themselves in the process.

TIP #46
KNOW WHEN TO READ
THE WRITING ON THE WALL

Sometimes changes occur above you, and you have no control over them. Maybe your supervisor leaves and is replaced by someone you don't know. Perhaps a senior level leader leaves the company, and a new executive takes over.

Sometimes these situations may work to your benefit, but sometimes they also work to your detriment as the new person looks to bring in their own hand-picked team. Knowing when it may be time to look elsewhere is critical. A move is not always required, but it pays to be aware of what is going on around you and how it may impact your career.

What are some of the signs that changes may not be in your favor? The following is certainly not an all-inclusive list, but some of the tell-tale signs can include:

• Suddenly not being included on a string of projects or other items you usually would have been involved in

• Being excluded from meetings where in the past you would have been a key participant

• Another individual is brought in to work alongside you and positioned as helping you, even though you didn't ask for help

• A lack of interest by your new boss in getting to know you on more than just a daily business level

We shouldn't judge these items in a vacuum but instead consider them in the entirety of the situation. As pointed out earlier, the grass isn't always greener somewhere else, but it does make sense to read the proverbial writing on the wall when it appears. Start to consider your options before the situation is forced upon you.

TIP #47
SOMETIMES LATERAL MOVES ARE OK!

I once had a lengthy discussion with a CPA that had become a CEO. One of the topics that came up was about a few lateral moves she had taken during her career. I found it interesting because many people think of lateral moves as limiting their growth, or as settling for something less than ideal. I asked her about the "why" behind these moves, and her response was insightful.

She believes we shouldn't judge a position strictly by title, pay, or even the size of the company, but we should instead holistically think about what the situation has to offer overall. Yes, characteristics of the company and position enter into the equation, but no one item is an overriding factor. A title may be lower than you have traditionally held, but the responsibilities in that position may be more significant. The company may be smaller, but the opportunity to learn may be better due to a broader breadth of responsibility. A job may even pay less than you are used to but still offer much more in terms of professional and personal growth opportunities.

The CEO's thought was that we should judge a position based on where we feel we could go with it if we dedicate our full effort to it. The holistic approach to weighing an opportunity made sense to me, and it has worked out well for the lady I was interviewing.

The next time you have an opportunity that appears to be a lateral move of sorts, judge it based on where you think the experience may lead versus where it seems to be right now. You may find yourself in a much better situation later on by making a change that appears to be "lateral" in the beginning.

TIP #48
DON'T BE AFRAID TO SAY
YOU DON'T KNOW THE ANSWER

Accounting is one of those professions where it is easy for us to think that we always need to have the answer for our clients, customers, or other individuals that trust us for our advice. After all, the reason they hire us is to help them with work that most people consider highly technical or complicated.

If you learn to admit when you don't have the answer or aren't 100% sure of the solution, you will find people appreciate your honesty and are willing to wait for the right answer. They will even appreciate you referring them elsewhere if that is the most appropriate option. People prefer any of those situations over receiving a response or solution they assume is right, only to find out the hard way that it was either entirely or partially incorrect.

Be willing to admit when you need time to research an issue, or even just think about it further. You will find that no one thinks less of someone who admits they don't know everything and cares enough to tell them the truth.

TIP #49
PRAISE IN PUBLIC, CORRECT IN PRIVATE

This tip is more for managers than specifically for accounting professionals, but it is still important as many of us aspire to be in leadership. One recurring theme you will find with accomplished managers is that they praise in public, sometimes frequently, but they always correct in private, with no exception.

These days, managers have responsibility for completing tasks beyond managing others. We have so much to do, it can be easy to become short-tempered and inappropriately correct team members in front of others.

There is no exception; you should never correct someone publicly. No matter how wrong they may be, or how correct you may be, it's never appropriate to correct in public. When you do, part of the individual's attention is focused on how others perceive them, which takes the attention away from improvement.

No matter how correct you may be, you will always come across as somewhat of a bully if you correct others publicly. Those of us standing by and observing the public correction will be naturally sympathetic to the corrected individual, if for no other reason than it's embarrassing and disrespectful to endure public correction.

If you always remember to correct in private, you will be more likely to see the behavior change you want. You will also be more respected as a manager, even by the person you are correcting. Praise in public and correct in private.

BONUS TIP #50
DO YOUR OWN TAXES...
AT LEAST UNTIL YOU'RE RICH

Sure, the world expects all accountants to be tax experts—though we all know that is not always the case! You likely have the ability to do taxes and the talent to understand them though, so why not at least keep in touch with those skills? If you do your own taxes, at least while they are relatively simple, it will keep you more in touch with your personal financial situation, and therefore make you a better advisor to others.

As your life becomes more complex, and as your tax situation perhaps follows suit, then seek professional help just as you would advise anyone else to do. While your tax situation is relatively basic though—W2s and other simple source documents—do your taxes yourself. You will benefit from your tax experience not only in your career, but in your overall financial life.

THE END . . . OR IS IT THE BEGINNING?

As I close out this book, I hope you have found value in some of the insights I've shared. Believe it or not, as I edit and re-edit the text, I find myself gaining additional insight into my own career journey.

My hope for you is that you either continue to be, or start to become, a life-long learner. I have been fortunate to have several key mentors in my career, and I'm thankful for every one of them. I hope you will always remain on the lookout for new individuals to learn something from.

Rather than simply close the book by wishing you well, I chose to provide a few items for you to think about as you move forward in your career journey.

Please take a few moments to answer the following questions. How can you apply some of the tips in this book to your life?

My best wishes to you in your life and career!

MARK GOLDMAN, CPA

ACTION ITEM #1

Which three tips could I benefit from applying to my own life and career?

1) _____

_____

_____

_____

2) _____

_____

_____

_____

3) _____

_____

_____

ACTION ITEM #2

What can I do <u>NOW</u> to work on the aspects or areas of my life and career where I would like to see improvement?

_____

_____

_____

_____

_____

_____

_____

_____

_____

_____

ACTION ITEM #3
30 days later . . .

What progress have I made? Be honest with yourself. Progress is progress!

_____

_____

_____

_____

_____

_____

_____

_____

_____

_____

_____

MARK GOLDMAN, CPA

Mark Goldman is a CPA and the founder of Where Accountants Go LLC, a career resource website for the accounting profession, and MGR Accounting Recruiters, a specialized recruiting firm in San Antonio, Texas.

Mark graduated from St. Mary's University, a private university located in San Antonio, Texas. He worked in public accounting handling tax and general business consulting, and then entered the employment industry in 1993. In 2007, he started the recruiting firm MGR Accounting Recruiters. In 2016, he started Where Accountants Go.

He has served in several professional associations at both the board level and committee level, including the Texas Society of CPAs, their local San Antonio Chapter, the Institute of Management Accountants, Financial Executives International, and the American Payroll Association. He also has led the career transition ministry at his church.

On a personal level, Mark was fortunate enough to be able to marry his high school sweetheart, Sayuki, and they are blessed with a wonderful family.

White Hart Publications is an imprint of Our Written Lives, LLC, and provides publishing services for authors in various educational and business organizations.

Visit our website for information and to submit your manuscript.

WWW.WHITEHARTPUBLICATIONS.COM